Author's Note

This books answers two key questions: How ANYONE can go on an adventure, and WHERE should you go? It doesn't matter if you go alone without a car on a tight budget, you can still have a wonderful adventure!!! Adventure comes in many forms: exploring cities, hiking through nature, or traveling the open road; my preference is traveling the open road. Even if you think you don't have the means to travel the country yet, don't put this book down yet, this book gives ANYONE the tools to go on an adventure with nearly ANY budget!! *I have made amazing daytrips count for $50 or less while making minimum wage, and I have driven through ½ of the states in the USA!!!* You can fly to get somewhere quickly, but I would suggest traveling by car, train or bus. I have found the best part of adventure is the journey, you would miss so much of the wonder and experience when you take a plane. <u>This guide will include:</u>

- Examples of traveling on a budget
- The costs you may face and how to best minimize them
- Whether you should travel in a group or by yourself
- How to make the trip **extra** fun!
- Awesome unique places to go in the USA
- We even talk about international travel

When I packed my car and moved across the country from Maine to Southern California, it was an out of this world adventure, one of my fondest memories! One of the most profound sights was watching the landscape slowly transform as I traveled between different regions of the country, it was as awe-inspiring as coastal California beaches, the majestic Rocky Mountains, and the towering Redwood forests. There is no right or wrong way to go adventure, but this book holds ideas from the wisdom I have gained from my many experiences across the country. I hope this book can bring you the same breathtaking level of happiness and adventure I've experienced and more!

Dedication

This guide is dedicated to my 1st car, my 2008 Buick Lacrosse. You have taken me from Southern Quebec to Tennessee to California, and you are still running!

Table of Contents

PART I - HOW Anyone Can Adventure

Chapter 1 - Introduction

Want to do something fun and different? Answer the call to adventure!! Adventure can consist of hiking through nature, traveling the open road, or exploring cities. I prefer traveling the open road, but *follow what you enjoy the most, pursue YOUR adventures! Try a local day trip to see for yourself if you like it.* "But my finances are tight..." you say, "I don't have a car..." you say...we can still make it happen! You can adventure with a tight budget; *I have made amazing daytrips count for $50 or less while making minimum wage!* Even when I did not have a car yet in Baltimore city, I'd take the light rail out of the city and explore the local stops by foot (or longboard). *Adventure truly is what you make of it, even if you're close to home!*

Part I of this book focuses on how ANYONE can go on an adventure, Part II presents the unique regions of the USA, the Epilogue introduces some international ideas, and the Afterward shares how I started my adventures (and what motivated me to write this book).

Part I includes successful examples, a breakdown of costs

(and how to best minimize them), the pros/cons of

traveling with a group or by yourself, and how to have

fun on your adventure. Anyone with nearly any budget

can go on an adventure, and there are so many unique

regions across the USA that are all worth visiting. Road

trips are my strong preference, especially since watching

the landscape slowly transform as you travel between

different regions across the country is a profoundly

sublime experience. Some of my fondest memories are

my road trips from Arkansas to New Mexico, Southern

California to Utah, and California's coastal roads leading

to the Redwood forests. Remember, *every person and

adventure are unique*, there are no set instructions for

how to adventure! I am simply sharing insight I have

gained from my experiences across the country from

Maine to California.

Chapter 2 – Examples of How to Travel on a Budget

I've included the following examples of various solo road trips I've taken at various budgets, even as low as $35!!! *This goes to show day trips are a great way to save money!* Having your own car helps with up-front costs, but the mileage and road conditions will eventually contribute to car repair costs. Therefore, I sometimes took an economy rental car instead of my own (ideally with high fuel efficiency). *Below are some examples of road trips* I've taken and their breakdown of costs, *notice how vehicle and lodging drive cost differences:*

1. Portland, Maine to White Mountains, New Hampshire: Daytrip - $35

   (2 hours of driving each way, 1 day of hiking/sightseeing)

   a. Water: $0 (from home)

   b. Food: $5 (1 Clif bar & 1 pack of turkey jerky)

c. Vehicle: My car

  i. $30 for gas (equipped with all-weather tires)

d. Tolls/Parking Fees: $0 (no tolls or parking)

e. Lodging: n/a

2. Maine to Southern Quebec: Daytrip - $50

   (4 hours of driving each way, 1 day of hiking/sightseeing)

   a. Water: $0 (from home)

   b. Food: $10 (3 Clif bars & 1 pack of turkey jerky)

   c. Vehicle: My car

      i. $40 for gas (equipped with all-weather tires)

   d. Tolls/Parking Fees: $0 (no tolls or parking)

   e. Lodging: n/a

3. Baltimore, Maryland to Harpers Ferry, West Virginia:

Daytrip - $120

(2 hours of driving each way, 1 day of

hiking/sightseeing)

    a. Water: $0 (from home)

    b. Food: $10 (2 Clif bars & 1 pack of turkey

        jerky)

    c. Vehicle:

        i. $80 for rental car

        ii. $30 for gas

    d. Tolls/Parking Fees: $0 (no tolls or

        parking)

    e. Lodging: n/a

4. Southern California to California Redwood Forests: 3

   Days - $680

   (12 hours of driving each way, 1 day of

   hiking/sightseeing)

        a.   Water: $0 (from home)

        b.   Food: $30 (6 Clif bars, 3 packs of turkey

             jerky, 3 apples, 3 oranges)

        c.   Vehicle:

             i. $200 for rental car

             ii. $150 for gas (gas in California is

                    no joke)

        d.   Tolls/Parking Fees: $0 (no tolls or

             parking)

        e.   Lodging: $300

Chapter 3 - Costs to Consider & How to Lower

This chapter will focus on ways to best mitigate costs, so you can road trip on a tight budget too! These are the key categories of costs you would face on a road trip:

1. Water

2. Food

3. Vehicle

4. Safety Gear

5. Tolls/Parking Fees

6. Lodging

Pro Tip: Set your budget ahead of time (so you know what you can and cannot afford).

Water

It is very important to stay hydrated, and you should NOT assume there will be access wherever you go. Don't fear though, this is a very easy and inexpensive thing:

1. Use a water filter at home to fill up your water bottles as many times as you want!

    a. For $3.33 a month you can get a 3 pack of filters that last for 6 months

    b. 3 packs typically cost $20, but last for 6 months

2. For $1, buy a 1-gallon jug of off-brand water

    a. You won't taste the difference, at least I don't!

Food

Shocking news, you need to eat too! My personal go to are CLIF Bars, Turkey Jerky, and PB&J sandwiches, here is why:

1. You don't have to worry about them going bad sitting in your daypack

2. They are especially great if you're out hiking, they give a lot of calories and protein

3. They taste delicious!

I can hear someone saying what about your health? Do not worry, for breakfast *before I head out, I always have my favorite mix of apples and oranges.* I do this so I can have them fresh and don't have to worry about storing my trash if I'm out hiking.

> _Pro Tip_: Tupperware is great to store trash.

Vehicle

When doing a road trip there are 3 options:

1. Use your own car

2. Rent a car

3. Use public transit (buses, trains, etc.)

Having access to a car will expand your access, but *if your budget is especially tight, there are plenty of adventures you can reasonably access by local buses, intercity buses or trains.* For $150 I've gotten an intercity bus between Maine and Maryland, that's 8-10 hours by car (with $100 in tolls if you were driving your own car).

Before you decide based on cost, *another key factor is to know the weather in your area!* If you're going somewhere hot, you're going to want your AC to be working. If you are going to the desert, you may want to keep your windows up during dust storms. If you are going somewhere that regularly snows, public transit can face delays and your car may need all weather or snow tires (with chains in mountain roads). I can attest I've gotten by just fine in snowy Maine with only all-weather tires without 4WD, but keep in mind I wasn't going out and driving in the middle of storms. Now if you decide you are going to take a car, *another key factor is gas.*

There are 2 things to consider:

1. Gas costs in your area
    a. I can say from experience gas in California and Nevada are almost double the price of the rest of the country
    b. These are wonderful areas to visit, you just need to budget more for gas is all

2. Number of travelers per car

    a. If you're traveling with a group in 1
        car, you all can split the cost of gas

    b. For example, a $80 rental car with
        $20 in gas for 4 people will only be
        $25 per person! That's way less than
        $100 by yourself!!

Safety Gear

Whether you take public transit or a car, you should have
the following safety gear in your daypack:

- Cell phone

- Food/water

- Flashlight

- Portable charger (with cord)

- Miniature first aid kit

- Spare socks/underwear

- Downloaded or Paper Map (in case you
  don't have cell service)

If you're taking a car, have the following in your trunk (whether it's yours' or a rental):

- First aid kit

- Winter clothing (in case you break down in cold weather)

- Spare tire

- Jumper cable

Quick Note on Safety

Safety gear is important, and wildlife is another equally important piece of safety to consider. I've been in different areas that have rattlesnakes, mountain lions, bears and moose. I've seen a few in person, but *I have never put myself in danger by following these rules!*

- Know ahead of time if there is any wildlife in the area you'll be traveling AND what type of animals to expect

- o   If you aren't already, *stay on trails*

- o   ***Know what to do*** just in case you run into dangerous wildlife

    - ▪ <u>*The key is to keep plenty of distance if you see them*</u>

Tolls/Parking Fees

<u>*If you're not bringing a car, you can skip to the next category on the next page.*</u> Depending on where you are traveling, you may run into toll roads and restrictions on parking. To save money, I do the following:

- • Avoid toll roads

    - o   If the detour is reasonable compared to the cost

        - ▪ For instance, detouring for hours to save $1 is probably not practical

- Avoid state parks with fees

    - Some fees are reasonable, but I've almost always gotten more from National Forests or Parks anyways (which are many times free and/or less expensive with a better payoff)

- Go to National Forests

    - In most cases these are completely free

- Go to National Parks

    - An annual National Park Pass is a high up-front cost, but pays for itself almost immediately

By following the above conditions, I've paid nearly nothing in tolls or parking fees (except for an Annual National Park pass, which is $80 per year).

Lodging

Good news, if you're doing a day trip, you can skip to the next chapter! ***But don't let cost deter you, there are many inexpensive ways to spend the night*** somewhere during your travels:

- Motels
    - I can personally attest motels can be nice, just conduct some prior research

- App Lodging (such as Airbnb)
    - May have options cheaper than motels/hotels
    - Many offer after hours self-check in
    - Keep in mind I've also found motels/hotels cheaper than Airbnbs, so field your options ahead of time

- Group Lodging

    - o All of you may be able to get a nicer place at a

       cheaper group rate

    - • For instance, when I traveled with my friends in

       Maine, we'd equally divide the Airbnb costs

- Cities

    - • If staying in a city, keep in mind there are

       usually a combination of well-developed and

       lesser developed areas. *For safety reasons, I'd

       advise sticking to the well-developed areas*

       (this comes from personal experience from

       living near a lesser developed city).

- Campgrounds

    - • These are wonderfully cheap compared to

       renting a room for the night

    - • You can sleep in a tent, RV, or even just a

       regular car

- Sleep in your car

    - It's not ideal, but I've power napped in my car once or twice before (I was doing 12 hours of driving that day roundtrip)

  - This depends of course *if you're allowed to park and accordingly sleep* in your car

  - Also, does the climate allow it? If it's freezing cold or burning hot, you should NOT be sleeping in your car!

  - Is it safe? If safety is even a slight concern, you'd probably be better off saving money for lodging that is safer.

Chapter 4 - Traveling Party: Group or Solo?

Do you need a group if you are going to road trip? Definitely not! I can say from experience that there are different pros and cons for traveling with a group or by yourself, but you don't have to pick just one. *I'd advise you <u>try both</u> traveling in a group and by yourself at least once, <u>find out which you prefer</u>!* But *remember, there is no right or wrong way to travel*, this section just highlights the limits and benefits of each.

Travel in a Group

I did a road trip of New England with close friends, and it is one of our fondest memories! We all shared a rental car and got a large Airbnb that was quite nice and cheap per person.

Pros

- One person isn't stuck driving the whole time

- Costs of a car can be shared (gas, rental fees, etc)

- Group rates may mean that you will individually pay less for lodging

- Sharing a trip can bring friendships closer than ever before

Cons

- Everyone must be in agreeance with the parties' plan
    - You may not be able to stop and see what you personally want to see
    - Your party will start the trip as soon as the last person is ready, *make sure they don't oversleep*
    - If you don't like anyone in your group, you'll be stuck with them for the duration of the trip (I am thankful I was never in this situation)

- Money can impede relationships, even shared planning/expenses with friends

  o   Evenly splitting things help a lot, but just be careful that no one feels slighted. _Remember, friendship is more important than anything else!_

Travel Alone

I've done many day trips by myself and it's a very different type of trip. It's more strenuous but also more freeing. As long as you're comfortable traveling on your own to new places, it's an option that is well worth considering and trying at least once.

Pros

- FREEDOM!!!

  o   You can leave as early as you want

  o   You can return as early as you want

  o   You can stop wherever you want

  o   You can change your route however you want

  o   You can listen to whatever music you want

Cons

- Safety

  o Can you drive by yourself, especially for long drives?

  o Are you comfortable traveling by yourself?

    - I've done many road trips by myself with no problems, but I still ALWAYS let someone know what I'm doing.

- Costs

  o Gas (and rental fees) for a car will be more expensive at an individual rate

  o Lodging will typically be more expensive at an individual rate

Chapter 5 – Don't Forget to Have Fun!

Here we are talking about planning and finances for your adventure, but there is a key element I'm forgetting: *Don't forget to have fun!* Here are some of my favorite things to do:

- Listen to your favorite music

- Stop to take in the scenery
  - Take pictures
    - You don't need a fancy DSLR camera, you can capture wonderful pictures from your phone!
    - If you like to draw, you can also draw as well, it's a quite meditative experience
  - If you have binoculars, stop at some vista points, and take in every inch of scenery!

- Talk with the locals!

    o   You don't truly know an area until you talk with the locals

        ▪ These can be simple short conversations like small talk

        ▪ By doing this I got invited onto my Airbnb hosts' private boat for the day, and we went to an island in Southern Quebec!

- Play your favorite musical instrument

    o   I enjoy brining my Kalimba since it's super portable and inexpensive

        ▪ There are great options online for less than $15

The key wisdom I'll share is that *adventure is an experience, it is what you make of it*. I've personally had trips where things didn't go as planned or just plain went wrong, but *you can choose whether or not you have fun!*

For instance, I was on the isolated part of the coastal California highway with gas stations nearly an hour away by car and part of the road was closed, so I had to turn around with a ¼ tank of gas. This was certainly stressful, but *instead of letting this bring me down, I just focused on what I had to do for safety, how I'd handle the worst outcome and had fun as I handled this new development.* The construction worker kindly redirected me to the nearest gas station, I enjoyed listening to my favorite music as I savored the beautiful sights of the Pacific Ocean heading to this gas station that helped me finish my reroute. My route was redirected by 3 hours, but that was 3 hours I wouldn't have had on this most scenic part of the coastal highway! I'm telling you, *it's all about that sweet silver lining!!!*

Brainstorm: How I am going to have fun?

(For best results, write in pencil so you can update as you wish)

1) _______________________________________

____

2) _______________________________________

____

3) _______________________________________

____

4) _______________________________________

____

5) _______________________________________

____

6) _______________________________________

____

7) _______________________________________

____

Chapter 6 - Recap

To quickly recap, this section has gone through how ANYONE can take an adventure via a road trip (my favorite and recommended method)! You can take a road trip, even if:

- Your budget it tight
- You don't have a car
- You go by yourself

There are many MANY ways to make this happen, regardless of your situation. Just plan it out ahead of time! So far, we've talked about:

- Examples of traveling on a budget
- The costs you may face (and how to best minimize these)
- The pros/cons to traveling in a group vs by yourself
- Making sure you have fun!

Now that you know HOW you can take an adventure, the next key question to answer is where; *Where should you go?* Part II will share ideas that help you decide where you should go, and then summarize the unique regions across the USA.

Before you continue to Part II, don't forget to use the following Brainstorm in the next page to help you plan your trip and manage costs!

Brainstorm: What Will My Adventure Cost?

(For best results, write in pencil so you can update as you wish)

Idea: _______________________________________

Budget: $_______

Water: $_______   _______________________________

Food: $_______   _______________________________

Vehicle: $_______   _______________________________

$_______   _______________________________

Tolls: $_______   _______________________________

Parking: $_______   _______________________________

Lodging: $_______   _______________________________

PART II – Where Should I Go?
Unique Regions of the USA

Chapter 7 – Where Should I Go?

There are many ways to decide where you should go, but *the simplest way to get your feet wet is to simply pull up a map and find what is close to you!* When I lived in Palm Springs California for instance, I first pulled up a map with my location and looked for what was near me. There I found wonderful hiking trails in the mountains at Idyllwild, the San Bernardino National Forest, and the Cleveland National Forest. *Even in the desert, I found nearby forests in the mountains!* How cool is that?! If you enjoy hiking, another great way to find places are to search for hiking trails near me with free mobile apps such as All Trails.

Brainstorm: Where Can I Adventure Near Me?

(For best results, write in pencil so you can update as you wish)

1) _______________________________________

____

2) _______________________________________

____

3) _______________________________________

____

4) _______________________________________

____

5) _______________________________________

____

6) _______________________________________

____

7) _______________________________________

____

You aren't tied down to only local areas though, consider the following:

- Are you able to get vacation time off for work?
  - The more time you have, the further you can travel and the more you can do
- Do you have friends/family in other parts of the country?
  - This can save you lodging costs
  - This can help mitigate your driving time per day
  - For example:
    - I've stayed the night at a friend's house in Maine once so I could travel to and from Northern Maine
    - This saved me from driving 11 hours roundtrip in 1 day
    - This also saved me from having to pay for lodging

Now that you have some ideas on where you can go, the remaining chapters will give a preview to the unique areas of the USA. These include:

- Pacific Northwest
- New England
- Yellowstone National Park
- Western Plateaus
- Southwestern Deserts
- Southeastern Swamps/Forests
- South Central Grasslands
- The Midwest
- Mountains
- Beaches

My personal favorites are the Pacific Northwest and New England but *visit everywhere and decide which is your favorite!*

P.S. I took majority of the pictures in this section myself! (excluding Yellowstone, Colorado and the Midwest since I haven't been there yet)

Brainstorm: Where Do I Want to Go in the USA?

(For best results, write in pencil so you can update as you wish)

1) _______________________________________

____

2) _______________________________________

____

3) _______________________________________

____

4) _______________________________________

____

5) _______________________________________

____

6) _______________________________________

____

7) _______________________________________

____

Chapter 8 - Pacific Northwest

I can share from personal experience that driving north on the coast from San Francisco into the redwood forests was one of my favorite routes of all time! I felt like no matter where I was, I was in those perfect pictures they show on your desktop!! It has rolling green hills, magnificent redwood forests, scenic flowers wherever you are, and beautiful coastal routes where you can see the Pacific Ocean from the cliffs or the beaches.

Gas is more expensive compared to the rest of the country, but it is well worth it to see this beauty! My personal recommendation if you don't live in Northern California is to fly into San Francisco (or Oakland), rent a car and drive north along the coast until you reach the redwood forests. I've attached a detailed list of stops I took:

1. San Francisco

2. Point Arena Lighthouse

3. Confusion Hill (for any fellow Gravity Falls fans)

4. Grandfather Tree

5. Humboldt Redwoods State Park (Free, inside "Avenue of the Giants")

    a. For the return journey, you can take the highway back and stop in the famous valley vineyards of Napa or Sonoma!

Photo: Point Arena Lighthouse

Photo: Confusion Hill

Chapter 9 - New England

New England is one of the most diverse and magical

places, especially in the fall with all of the fall foliage!

That isn't only my personal experience talking though,

when I lived in Portland, Maine I was:

- Equidistant to Boston and the White

  Mountains in New Hampshire

- Close to many towns in Coastal Maine

- Driving distance to Cape Cod, Vermont,

  Northern Maine & Southern Quebec

There are many places to explore from mountains to beaches, listed are some of my favorites:

- The White Mountains, New Hampshire
  - Franconia Notch in the fall was one of my favorite trails
    - You will see fall conditions in the lower half of the mountains, but the peaks face full winter conditions (it's a sublime sight)
    - *Pro Tip:* This trail is packed with people in the weekends, but much less crowded in the weekdays
- Acadia National Park
  - A unique park like no other, an island that has beaches, mountains, and cliffs!
  - If possible, visit on a weekday. Parking is very limited in the weekends.

- Boston Harbor Islands

    o   You can take a ferry from Boston to various nearby islands

    o   If you like history, check out Georges' Island, a military base used during the Civil War!

- Cape Cod

    o   Want to play in some sand dunes by the ocean? Check out Dune Shacks Trail!

        ▪   If you hike for a little bit, you'll have a wonderful view of the ocean from a remote beach with very few people around

- Baxter State Park

    o   My 1st 4000' mountain summit was here at Mount Katahdin, this is a very popular gem of Northern Maine!

    o   Reserve parking ahead of time, spots fill VERY quickly

Chapter 10 – Yellowstone National Park

Photo Credit: Enlin Lee via Unsplash.com

When you hear about nature and national parks, Yellowstone will be one of the first names you hear, and for good reason! This park is located within the following states in the Northwest: Montana, Wyoming & Idaho. This a massive national park covering a big area with many things to do, these are the top things I plan to do when I can finally visit:

- See the geysers (particularly the famous "Old Faithful")

- Hike in the Grand Teton National Park

- View the Grand Canyon of Yellowstone from the famous overlook "Artist's Point"

This area is quite remote from majority of the country, so if you're flying in like I will, fly into:

- *Bozeman, MT (probably my first choice,* near airport with reasonably priced tickets)

- West Yellowstone (local airport, but more expensive tickets on average)

- Salt Lake City (if you don't mind driving for a while for cheaper tickets)

Chapter 11 - Colorado

Photo Credit: Joshua Woroniecki via Unsplash.com

Colorado is another place well known for its' natural beauty and access to the Rocky Mountains. There are surprisingly diverse natural features including mountains, forests, and rivers as well as plateaus, deserts, and canyons. In such a big and diverse place there are SO many things to do, these are the places I'll be going when I can visit:

- Rocky Mountain National Park

- Great Sand Dunes National Park and Preserve

- Garden of the Gods Visitor and Nature Center

- Mesa Verde National Park

Everyone I've met who has visited Colorado has nothing but wonderful things to say, I know I'd like to see this place for myself!

Chapter 12 - Western Plateaus

One of the most interesting day trips I took was a day trip between Southern California and Zion National Park in Utah. During this drive I saw the desert slowly evolve into picturesque plateaus, definitely a sight to see for yourself! The climate was also quite interesting, it was intriguing to see more rocks than trees in a cooler climate.

Plateaus can be found in the following states:

- Utah

- Wyoming

- Colorado

- Arizona

- New Mexico

Chapter 13 – Southwestern Deserts

Deserts are unique compared to the rest of the country, I have driven from Northern Texas to Southern California and Southern California to Eastern Nevada. There are not many trees there sure, but there are many beautiful flowers and plants you will not see anywhere else. You can also find unique wildlife too, just be sure to leave dangerous wildlife alone (especially Mojave Rattlesnakes). I can tell you it's a very different experience from forests and grasslands, and even if you don't like it, it's very cool the first few times you see it!

<u>_Pro tip:_</u> Shield yourself from the sun with a hat, and light breathable long sleeves and pants. Also be ready for the nights to be significantly colder than the days, check the weather forecast before you pack!

There are so many places you can explore depending on your location, listed are simply some of my most memorable:

- Coconino National Forest, Arizona
    - You want to see something amazing? How about a dense lush forest in the middle of the desert?! I was driving from New Mexico to Southern California, and I was shocked to suddenly be driving through forests as far as the eye could see (for a few hours)!!
- Idyllwild, California
    - Speaking of forests in the middle of the desert, this local mountain town 6000' feet from the desert floor has its own temperate climate. I can personally attest it is a wonderful preview of what Northern California is like.

- Petrified Forest National Park, Arizona

  o This badland used to be filled with trees millions

    of years ago, but these trees fossilized. Hence the

    name "Petrified Forest"

- Spring Mountains, Nevada

  o These mountains are quite interesting, very vivid

    segmented colored rocks and mountains, one of

    the mountains is literally called the Rainbow

    Mountain!

  o If you drive there from Southern California, you

    get to:

    - Go through the Mojave Desert

    - See Las Vegas

    - Drive through some local desert towns that

      try to be a mini Las Vegas

    - The Ivanpah Solar Generating tower that

      looks like a lighthouse in the middle of the

      desert at night!

Chapter 14 – Southeastern Swamps/Forests

The further south you go, the climate and environment

shift more from temperate forests to humid swamps. I've

driven from New Jersey to Orlando Florida, and it's

quite intriguing to see the temperate forests morph into

swampy forests. New Jersey will see snowy winters, but

Floridian winters can face average highs of 75 F humid

heat, it was mind boggling to me!

> *Pro tip, you can always visit the southeast in the*
>
> *winter like I do, this way humidity doesn't mean*
>
> *intense heat!*

Don't let my preferences dissuade you though from your potential adventures, you can have plenty of fun in the summer too.

There are a lot of historical attractions and sites in the Southeast. Even if you're not a history buff, it can still be TONS of fun (especially in Washington D.C., FREE Smithsonian museums)!! There are also prominent cities from New York City all the way to Miami Florida, beaches spanning the east coast, swamps within/near Florida, and lastly the Appalachian Mountains (home to many national forests and parks).

Chapter 15 - South Central Grasslands

In this area you can see the land go through many distinct transformations. Driving from Tennessee to Oklahoma you could see the land change from humid forests to temperate fields of grass and flowers to temperate farmlands. It was amazing watching the land go through all of these transitions in a days' drive!

I personally loved that drive from Arkansas to Oklahoma, you could see the most beautiful fields of grass and flowers (2nd only to the Pacific Northwest Coast). My travels were limited to predominantly Route

40 but did include some detours such as a free state park (Lake Thunderbird, Oklahoma), and a vineyard I found by accident near that beautiful field in Arkansas called Wiederkehr Village Wine & Spirits. This is a region I certainly want to visit again and spend more time in, my first stop will probably be the Ozark & Ouachita National Forests in Arkansas.

Chapter 16 –The Midwest

Photo Credit: Vincent Ledvina via Unsplash.com

I have close friends that have nothing but wonderful things to say about the Midwest, they grew up in Minnesota and Wisconsin. I personally haven't seen it myself yet, but I'm including their praise of the area since they're also well-traveled adventurous types who speak highly of this area. I can at least say that I have been to downtown Chicago and that is a wonderful city to visit (I've been to cities across the USA, and this is quite a unique one).

Pro tip, their deep-dish pizzas are no joke, get ready to loosen your belt!! Chicago aside, these are the places I will be visiting as soon as I get the chance:

- Northern Lights
    - You can see the northern lights from various places in Minnesota, Wisconsin, and Michigan
- Superior National Forest, Minnesota
    - Giant forest with over 2,000 lakes and streams that borders Canada and Lake Superior, talk about too many options!
- Sleeping Bear Dunes National Lakeshore, Michigan
    - Giant sand dunes you can climb that overlooks the giant Lake Michigan? Sounds like quite a lot of fun to me!
- Mount Rushmore, South Dakota
    - You know that place with all those president heads carved into a mountain?!

- Fall Foliage

    - I don't know if this region can compare to New England's picturesque fall foliage, but I plan to see this for myself!

- Mall of America

    - Giant mall known across the USA. I mean why not, right?

Chapter 17 - Mountains

I've been to mountains all across the country at islands, deserts, plateaus, and forests. There is no feeling like summiting a mountain and watching everything from the heavens, summiting mountains are definitely underrated! Plus, if you enjoy cooler weather like I do, mountains will usually be cooler due to their higher elevation and wind chill. For instance, San Bernadino is a town 1,000' from sea level in Southern California, and one of their mountains' called Sugarloaf is almost 10,000'. They respectively face average temperatures in May of 82 -

54 F versus 56 -24 F. To be fair though, I was always around forests and beaches as a kid, but never mountains, so I may be a tad biased. Joking aside, go and see things you haven't seen yet, it could be your next favorite thing (like mountains are for me).

Chapter 18 - Beaches

There is nothing more soothing than listening to waves

hitting the shore, especially when you're there in person

to feel the sand between your toes!! Beaches are very

popular though, so if you're introverted like I am, look

out for remote beaches (or at least remote parts of a

beach). It can be MUCH more relaxing when you get out

of the crowd! I've personally found remote beaches in

Northern California, Maine, and Massachusetts. Those

remote beaches were far better than Southern California,

New Jersey and Ocean City Maryland, these are very

popular places known for their beaches, so they are also

typically overcrowded. Regardless, see these places for

yourself and find what you like the most, it's your

adventure after all!

Chapter 19 - Recap

This section briefly went through the many different areas you can find across the USA. I propose you *get your feet wet by first visiting something new that is close to you, then visit everywhere when you can!* The goal isn't to get somewhere specific, but to enjoy the journey and find what you'd like to experience more of!! My personal favorites are the Pacific Northwest, New England, and Yellowstone National Park, but there are many areas in the USA:

- Pacific Northwest
- New England
- Yellowstone National Park
- Western Plateaus
- Southwestern Deserts
- Southeastern Swamps/Forests
- South Central Grasslands
- The Midwest
- Mountains
- Beaches

There are many unique regions in the USA, and *even those outside of your inherent preferences have more awes to offer then you'd probably expect.* For instance, the desert is one of my least favorite regions, but I was surprised at how beautiful and various the desert flora is. Words cannot properly describe how profound and exciting it was to see a completely different area for the first time and explore it!!

The beginning of this book focused on how ANYONE can make an adventure happen, and the current section highlighted unique regions in the USA to determine where to go first (before ideally visiting everywhere). ***Don't stop reading yet though, the epilogue and afterward share some important content and insight!*** The epilogue shares some ideas for those fortunate enough to travel internationally, and the last section of this book ties it all together with a brief afterward. This afterward reflects on how I started my adventures which highlights what I learned and what motivated me to write this book!

Before that though, remember when you brainstormed

ideas of where you want to go? Write down any new

ideas here!

New Ideas: Where Do I Want to Go in the USA?

(Write in pencil so you can update as you wish)

1) ____

____

2) ____

____

3) ____

____

4) ____

____

5) _______________________________

____

6) _______________________________

____

7) _______________________________

____

Epilogue – Where Should I Go? International Ideas

As I'm writing this, I've adventured internationally to Quebec City, Canada and Mexico. It was amazing to visit Quebec City and explore its' history while also traveling outside the city for various hiking trails. I lived in Maine at the time, so it was very feasible to drive there and stay a few nights locally. International travel usually isn't so convenient though, flights are typically required which raises travel costs by a lot. When the time comes that I gain disposable income, these are the places I plan to travel to:

- Japan
- Iceland
- New Zealand
- Chile
- Northern European countries
- European countries near the Alps

The listed countries are simply my suggestions, remember that you can choose anywhere you want though! *Follow what you enjoy the most, pursue YOUR adventures!* These countries are in no particular order, it'll depend on your proximity, finances, opportunities, and personal preferences. There are many more countries across the world, but these are the ones I've selected due to my personal preferences that include: environmental wonders, diverse landscapes, rich culture, high rank from other adventurers

Now that I've shaved my international ideas, brainstorm

where you would want to travel outside of the USA!

*Brainstorm: Where Do I Want to Travel
Internationally?*

(For best results, write in pencil so you can update as you wish)

1) __________________________________

____

2) __________________________________

____

3) __________________________________

____

4) __________________________________

____

5) ________________________________

____

6) ________________________________

____

7) ________________________________

____

I've written in a little bit of what I know about each

place I've suggested to show why I chose those countries

in particular:

Japan

Photo Credit: David Edelstein via Unsplash.com

- From Okinawa in the south to Hokkaido in the north, there is so much more to Japan than just the capital city of Tokyo.

- There are many diverse regions across the country that include mountains, forests, beaches, and even a desert!

- Culture isn't only profoundly rich here; it is also unique to only this location.

- Travel is a cinch here; Japan has a wonderful system of trains that can take you all across the country with ease!!

- If you've ever watched a Hayao Miyazaki film, I don't need to say much to convince you that Japan has many diverse regions that are each beautiful in their own special way.

- Speaking of Japanese animation, if you're into anime like I am, then enjoy this place where majority of anime comes from and draws inspiration from!

Iceland

Photo Credit: Jonathan Ybema via Unsplash.com

- This little island has many diverse landscapes too, including amazing fjords, hot springs, lava landscapes, waterfalls, steaming fields, and Europe's largest glacier!

- There is also a rich culture including food, the arts, and their Nordic history.

- Bonus, you can see the northern lights here!

New Zealand

Photo Credit: Kuno Schweizer via Unsplash.com

- This island has a very diverse environment of high elevation mountain ranges, forests, grasslands, wetlands, and coastlands.

- For anyone who has seen the Lord of the Rings movie trilogy, this was the filming location due to its' diverse environments.

Chile

Photo Credits: *Tyler Gooding & Olga Stalska*
(via Unsplash.com)

- The city of Santiago has friendly people and a rich culture including art, cuisine, and wine.

- The further south you go from the city of Santiago, the more parks and wonderful natural features you'll find!

- This countries' picturesque natural features include mountains, lakes, volcanoes, and fjords.

    o No wonder there are so many national parks here!

Norway: A Northern European Country

Photo Credit: Andreas M via Unsplash.com

- Almost all of my favorite pictures of snowy mountains are sourced from Norway, this country is definitely at the top of my list!

- Majority of this country borders the ocean, so there are many beautiful port towns!

- Their culture includes Nordic history, food, and the arts.

- You can see the northern lights from here too!

- Bonus: Norway neighbors Sweden and Finland, so if time allows, these places could certainly be worth visiting as well.

European Countries near the Alps

Photo Credit: Patrick Robert Doyle via Unsplash.com

The famous European mountain range the Alps are found in the following countries: Germany, Austria, Switzerland, Italy, France, Slovenia and Liechtenstein.

- Each of these are different countries, so you'll find very different cultures and cities in very close proximity!

- Once you fly in, you can travel between countries by train or budget friendly transit.

There are obviously many more countries in Europe, but I'm going to review the following due to proximity, environmental preferences, history, and personal preferences:

- *Germany*
    - I have friends that lived or visited Germany and they have nothing but wonderful things to say about the culture, natural features, people, history, and the cars too!
    - Just search "Germany Landscapes", it sells itself VERY easily!
- *Austria*
    - Quite similar to Germany, this country has rich culture, natural features, and history
    - For any fans of the classic movie "The Sound of Music", it took place in Austria

- *Switzerland*
  - o This country is famous in many things from their scenic villages, high peak mountain-tops, the Swiss Army Knife, chocolates, and cheeses (to name a few)
    - ▪ In fact, over half of the country includes the high-peak Alps!
- *Italy*
  - o This country is well known for its cuisine, culture, history, and natural features
  - o Known as one of the cuisine capitals of the world, especially pizzas and pastas
  - o Bonus, you can visit Vatican City too!
- *France*
  - o There is more to France than just fine dining and couture in Paris, there are beautiful lavender fields, country sides, and mountains as well!

Recap

International travel and selecting locations will depend on your proximity, finances, opportunity, and personal preferences. The suggestions I've provided include my personal preferences of environmental wonders, diverse landscapes, rich culture, and high rank from other adventurers. *Now the key is to save up enough money to visit these amazing countries and more!* Keep in mind you don't have to follow my suggestions, the key is to *follow what you enjoy the most, pursue YOUR adventures!* Lastly, the afterward shares my story that highlights what I learned and what motivated me to write this book. Don't forget to write down any new ideas here!

New Ideas: Where Do I Want to Travel Internationally?

(Write in pencil so you can update as you wish)

1) _______________________________________

____

2) _______________________________________

____

3) _______________________________________

____

4) _______________________________________

____

5) _______________________________________

____

6) _______________________________________

____

7) _______________________________________

____

Afterward - How I Started My Adventures

Many of my fondest memories are from my many adventures across the USA, especially my biggest adventure of moving from Maine to Southern California by car. Since I was learning, my adventures didn't have the smoothest start, but *after reading this book, you should have a smooth ride!* This afterward will share the highlights of my story to walk you through how my adventures started.

Before I even knew what adventure was as a kid, I would be running around aimlessly in the woods at the river we lived near in Maryland. My family didn't take many trips outside of the occasional trips to beaches in New Jersey or annual trips out of state, but these focused on the typical vacation experience instead of adventure. These trips were fun and I had a wonderful time, it just was not the same as the adventures my heart has always sought. Once I moved out to Baltimore City for college, this was where I started my search for adventure without even realizing it! *I didn't have a car, but regularly used public transit. As I became more familiar with public transit, I gained more freedom to go wherever I wanted.* When I was not at school or work, I'd take my longboard and ride the light rail into downtown or far away from the city all together. *Even if it was just local, I have always enjoyed experiencing new things and new places!*

Once I got my drivers' license a few years later, I could finally rent a car for the day and visit so many more places! My first trip was a day trip between Baltimore, Maryland and Harpers Ferry, West Virginia, this was the start of my many amazing road trips to come! Shortly after I was introduced to my partner in crime, my grandfather's old car!! Who knew this car was going to adventure with me all across the country, I would never have guessed! Anyways, now that I had a partner in crime, we could now regularly visit my grandfather and aunt in Northern New Jersey. *Even on a bad day, there was a profound serenity on the road*

going to and from!

After my car and I got to know each other

better, it was time to take him on his first big trip,

Maryland to Maine!! Once I knew he was ready for the

trip, we moved to Maine to start my Master's in graduate

school, and nothing was going to stop us from

adventuring! In New England, we ventured far further,

found far greater adventures, and created the most

profound memories. Some senior students invited us to

the magnificent island of Acadia National Park, this was a

big eye opener for someone who didn't get to explore

much nature outside of Maryland yet! I then took the key

leap of faith and took a day trip by myself to Mount

Katahdin in Baxter State Park, the very first mountain I

summited and one of my most truly ethereal experiences.

I still vividly remember hiking up in the cold rain and

reaching the summit covered in rain clouds, but as I

descended, I saw the clouds open the curtain to the most

picturesque mountain views for as far as the eye could

see. After this experience, I got my best friends in Maine to join me in trips all over New England: the White Mountains of New Hampshire, the perfect fall foliage of Vermont, the beaches of Cape Cod, the city of Boston with its' harbor islands, and the easternmost point of the USA in Lubec Maine. They are an outstanding group of people that are a riot too, this made our travels as a group a LOT of fun! I remember one of them would always race down the mountains like a daredevil, but never get a scratch, it was amazing! Another would always make us laugh with his sense of humor and silly poses in front of the camera. Another was the best cook, he actually helped teach me how to cook! Lastly, the other was so kind and sweet, he would always make our days that much better! I could go on and on and on about how great each of them are in every way, but the key is every one of them are true gems and we always had so much fun going on adventures together!!

I enjoyed the time to myself when traveling alone, but I would've missed something great if I didn't *also travel with companions. **Why choose one or the other when you can have both?!*** In this spirit, I later went alone on a wonderful road trip in Southern Quebec where I visited Quebec City as well as 3 wonderful hiking trails, one of my Airbnb hosts even invited me on a boat trip with their family! They had their own boat, so we went along a river surrounded by trees to a little private island. There was a little forest here, some kayakers passing by and the most picturesque views of nature!

Shortly after, the perfect girl named Parivash came along, and she changed EVERYTHING! Since the start we have been deeply in love, so when she visited family in Chicago, I offered to visit Chicago with her (and did)! This was a wonderful trip that I likely would not have taken if she wasn't there. When we graduated school together the following year, she moved to Southern California for work. We were apart for about half a year, but then I got approval to work from home, so then my car and I began the ultimate journey, moving to Southern California to be with my perfect girl! *My trip from Maine to Southern California covered 19 states in 5 days, 12 hours of driving per day! It was exciting, exhausting and the epitome of adventure, I would do it all over again every single time if I could!! It was amazing to watch forests slowly change into grassy plains and then fade into deserts, you truly need to see it for yourself!!*

This covered the following states: ME, NH, MA, CT, NY, NJ, PA, MD, WV, VA, TN, KY, MO, AR, OK, TX, NM, AZ, CA. My poor old sedan survived driving from the east coast to the west coast, literally ocean to ocean! Along this trip I made so many palpable memories, starting with Shenandoah National Park in Virginia. The road quickly ascended the mountains and then you were driving along the mountain tops with the most scenic views of the forests below! Later that day, I entered Tennessee and it was so humid that if I turned off my AC, my car's air vents literally brought in water, this was so unexpected and funny to me! Then came Arkansas, I don't think I've seen such a beautiful grassy field of flowers anywhere else, watching them dance in the wind was so serene!! I also remember how profoundly comfortable each of the motels I stayed in for the night were, especially this little motel in a truck stop in Oklahoma. They were so cozy and comfy, a very welcome place to rest after 12 hours in the car!! New Mexico and Arizona were quite unexpected too; after driving a while through the desert I was shocked to see large forests in the middle of the desert. Once you were inside these forests, all you could see were trees, you didn't even know you were in the desert anymore (for a few hours at least)!! Before I knew it, I finally landed in California, oh my what an adventure!

Now that I lived in Southern California, I took ***full advantage of where I was and visited beaches*** *in San Diego, the* ***towering mountains*** *of Idyllwild and San Bernardino,* ***and nearby deserts*** *in California and Nevada.* The best part was sharing these memories with Parivash, especially when I proposed to her in an A-Frame cabin in Idyllwild! After becoming well acquainted with Southern

California I gave my old sedan some rest and rented a slick BMW to venture out into Utah, this was quite an interesting day trip indeed! We drove through the Mojave Desert to the Spring Mountains near Las Vegas, and then to Zion National Park. *The desert may be barren, but seeing it slowly morph into colorful segmented mountains and then into plateaus was a very interesting sight indeed!* It was amazing to see mountains and plateaus with bright layers of red, orange, yellow and brown. The mountain towns of Idyllwild and San Bernardino in Southern California were a wonderful preview of the climate and environment of Northern California, but I have always dreamed of seeing it in person. So, I accordingly picked up a part time job, saved some money, rented a car, and had the most wonderful trip to the Pacific Northwest!! I took my time driving up along the coast which eventually led into the Redwood forests, all that time driving was absolutely worth it. Out of all of my trips, this was the penultimate adventure by far, (second only to when Parivash could join me)!

The best thing of all is that this isn't where my adventures

end, this is only the beginning of many to come!!!